TABLE OF CONTENTS

CHAPTER 1. HOW TO TELL IF YOUR DOG IS SMART

What are the traits of a smart dog?

- ### Curiosity

Dogs who are curious about anything and everything. They like to explore. To peak in containers to look what's inside. To climb over ledges and barriers to see what's on the other side. Smart dogs make things happen, to find out what things do once they bump it with their paw or nose. They like to play with random objects, they like to taste it. They like to follow noises and track it down to see where it came from. They have an inquisitive mind.

- ### Keen Observation Skills

Smart dogs observe you, your facial expressions, and your body language and interpret your moods. They learn from observing. And not just from observing you personally, but also from observing other dogs. If they see another dog doing something that earns them a reward, they may try it themselves in order to see if they get the same reward. Smart dogs listen to conversations in order to pick out familiar words out of complex sentences.

- ### Fast Learning

Intelligent dogs only need to be shown new things a few times and they simply get it. New behaviors and words will be picked up after only a few hours of training.

- ### Solid Memory

Not only do they learn new behaviors or words fast, smart dogs remember.

Once they have learned something new, you don't need to go over it again and again.

- ## Flexibility

Smart dogs are creative. They come up on their own with new ideas and techniques until it works. Playing this 'trial and error' shows their intelligent creativity so they don't get stuck doing the same thing over and over again.

CHAPTER 2. HOW TO TELL IF YOUR DOG ISN'T SO SMART

The traits of a not-so-smart dog

• Contentment

Lesser intelligent dogs lack curiosity. Once presented with new objects like toys or a new environment, they aren't interested in exploring it. They are generally satisfied with how things are and are content with everything.

• Limited Observation

Slower dogs are mostly oblivious to your body language or facial expressions. They won't notice if you stick your tongue out, make a funny face or smile at them. They simply don't learn from observation eve if they watch other dogs do something for rewards and they will not repeat it themselves unless it's specifically shown to them over and over again. Nor do they pay attention to conversations or listen in in order to fins specific words in sentences.

• Slow Learning

Before none intelligent dogs start to 'sit' or 'lay down' or 'stay', they need many repetitions before they actually understand what you're trying to make them do. Often it takes 25 or more repetition before they grasp the concept of it.

• Short memory

Similarly to slow learning, they may even forget what they've been thought a day before. Unless you practice it frequently and often.

• Fixed Habits

Some not-so-smart dogs do not come up with new techniques for solving a problem. They don't play 'trial and error' and will generally get stuck trying the same thing over and over again even though it will get them nowhere. They are neither creative nor flexible enough to try new ways.

After reading these descriptions on smart and not so smart dogs, you may already have an understanding on how smart your dog actually is. Let's find out if you're right and test this.

CHAPTER 3. TESTING YOUR DOG'S IQ

The IQ Test measures five thing:

- **Learning ability.** How quickly your dog can learn new behaviors and words.
- **Solving problems.** How persistent or clever your dog is by trying to find a solution to a problem in order to gain some sort of reward.
- **Observation.** How observant your dog is to your moods, facial expressions and changes in his environment.
- **Memory.** Testing your dog's memory and see how long it takes to remember what he has learned, heard or seen.
- **Curiosity.** To see how interested your dog is trying something new.

The rules

Do only a few tests at the time. There are 25 in total and doing them all at once might overwhelm and exhaust your dog and the score will gradually become lower and lower due to fatigue. On top of that, he will also become less motivated because he'll be full on treats!

My advice is to do a few in the morning and a few in the evening and another few in the afternoon. But do all the IQ tests in the span of two or three days. That way you will be giving your best friend a fair chance to get the highest score as possible since for each group of tests, he will be well rested and mentally as sharp as a knife. And perhaps a bit hungry and more motivated because of that.

Use soft treats

I personally recommend softer treats as reward for the tests. Something with a strong smell for example. Cheese or cooked chicken also works. If you know from experience that food doesn't work at all on your dog, perhaps use a ball or favorite toy instead.

Plan ahead

If a test requires you to build something, please do so ahead of time. Same goes for materials you might need like a soup can or towels or whatever. Gather them beforehand. Your treats should be cut in small squares if at all possible. Should you require a helper, make sure that person is available. Have everything ready so that when you get your dog in order to start the tests, you can run through them without needing a pause while you still have your dog's enthusiasm and full attention.

Do not repeat tests

For scoring purposes, do not repeat tests. Only the first time doing the test will truly reflect your dog's innate abilities. Should something unusual happen like the doorbell ringing or children bursting in on the test or something falling that frightens your dog, you should abandon the test until everyone has calmed down and had a chance to regroup. Then repeat it again. But do not repeat a test in hopes for a higher score.

You will notice that I don't want you to repeat a test for a better score, you are however encouraged to repeat a test just for fun. In fact, if your dog does a poor job on the test or cannot do it at all, you are strongly encouraged to help him before you go on to the next test. Your dog will benefit greatly from these new skills he learns in accomplishing each test, whether his score is low or high.

Make it a game

I cannot emphasize this enough. Encouragement for your dog to do his best, no matter what he does makes it an enjoyable game for him. Give him smiles, a hug, a cheerful pat. Simply treat the IQ test as an enjoyable game for both you and your dog.

TEST 1

Goal of the test:

To measure your dog's initiative and problem solving skills. Will we find out if your dog can find out where you are hiding and will he come to you even if he has to push his way through an obstacle?

Things you need:

- A helper
- A table covered in blankets or cloth

Do the Test:

1. While your dog is confined in another room, cover the table with blankets or a large cloth that hang just to the floor, forming a dark "cave" under the table. The table itself must be large enough for you to sit under.
2. Crawl under the table, making sure the blankets or cloth are hanging on to the floor.
3. Your helper at this point should bring your dog into the room with the table and you underneath it. Once your helper has notified you that he is in the room with your dog, call your dog's name and encourage him to come to you. Your helper should then release your dog and start the timer.

Scoring:

If you dog managed to push his way under the blankets within 15 seconds: **Score 5**

If he is frantically trying to get to you, running around and around the table

and making an effort to breach the blanket or cloth, but not quite able to bring himself to do so within 60 seconds:
Score 2

If he only makes a mild effort to get through the blankets or cloth:
Score 1

If he makes no attempt to get through the blankets or cloth within 60 seconds, or if he walks away:
Score 0

TEST 2

Goal of the test:

Measuring the problem-solving skills of your dog. What will he do when his water bowl is empty and he is thirsty?

Things you need:

- Your dog's water bowl or dish (empty)

Do the test:

1. Make sure your dog's water bowl is empty and take him either on a good long walk or play energetically with him. You want him to be thirsty.
2. After the walk or play, keep your eye on him to see when he goes to his water bowl. What does he do when he finds it empty?

Scoring:

If your dog comes to you and barks, paws at you, leads you to his water bowl or even brings the bowl to you.
Score 3. He clearly knows you are the source of his water.

If he starts looking for another source of water, like a puddle in the yard or even toilet.
Score 3. He is self-sufficient although drinking out of the toilet might not be desirable.

If he paws at the bowl, nudges it, pushes it, flips it or barks at it.
Score 2. He is actively trying to make water appear, but not sure where it

comes from.

If he waits in silent near his bowl, hoping water magically appears.
Score 1.

If your dog does absolutely nothing or just walks away.
Score 0.

TEST 3

Goal of the test:

We will be testing your dog's response to human social signals. Will he recognize your facial expressions and body language when you act as though you hear something suspicious? Will he join in?

Things you need:

- One relaxed, lying down dog
- Your Oscar performance worthy acting skills

Do the test:

1. Watch for a time when your dog is relaxed and either sitting or lying down (but not sleeping).
2. When your dog looks at you, suddenly stop what you're doing and pretend you hear something and look towards the door or window. Move to peer out the door or window and tilt your head the way you do when you hear something. Move your head and eyes in tiny little movements in different direction the way you do when you're trying to zero in on a source of strange sounds.
3. While trying to listen to these imaginary sounds, don't look at your dog. Just observe him from the corner of your eye.

Scoring:

If you dog immediately starts to bark or run to the windows or doors. **Score 3.** He is very attentive.

If he raises his head and listens as though he's trying to hear what you're

hearing, but hold his sitting or lying down position.
Score 2.

If he gives you an inquisitive look, but doesn't not really listen or otherwise mimic any suspicion that you might have.
Score 1.

If he doesn't react at all.
Score 0.

TEST 4

Goal of the test:

Measuring your dog's curiosity and attentiveness. Will he actually investigate strange sounds or noises?

Things you need:

- A sleeping dog
- A pen or pencil

Do the test:

1. When your dog is sleeping, relaxed and comfortable at least ten feet (3 meters) away from you.
2. Without looking at your dog but watching him from the corner of your eyes, start making repetitive sounds such as the tapping of the pen or pencil slowly but rhythmically on your table or desk. Keep this up for a full 30 seconds.

Scoring:

If your dog comes over to check out the sounds.
Score 4.

If he raises his head in order to listen to the sounds intently, but doesn't come over to check it out.
Score 3.

If he raises his head and listens intently to the sounds for a few seconds and then puts his head back down to ignore it.
Score 2.

If he indicates that he hears the sound by either flicking or moving his ear, opening his eyes or moving his body but shows no real interest.
Score 1.

If he doesn't react at all.
Score 0.

TEST 5

Goal of the test:

Let's see how good your dog's memory is. It will test their memory and initiative. Does he remember that a treat exists even when they can no longer see it? Will he actively try and search for it?

Things you need:

- One treat
- A helper

Do the test:

1. Have your helper hold your dog while you crouch or kneel a couple of feet away. Show your dog the treat. Tuck the treat into your closed fist and let your dog sniff it for a good few seconds so your dog will get excited about the treat.
2. Slowly but deliberately put your fist behind your back, making sure your dog sees this movement. Rest your empty hand on your leg, palm down.
3. Your helper will then release your dog and start a timer. You strongly encourage your dog to then find the treat.

Scoring:

If the dog immediately runs behind your back, nuzzling your closed hand. **Score 5**

If your dog checks out your front and empty hand first, or sniffing your leg after which he finds his way behind your back and nuzzling your closed hand containing the snack within 30 seconds.

Score 4

If your dog makes it behind your back but keeps sniffing around your body, not realizing the treat is in your hand for 30 seconds.
Score 3

If your dog stays in front of you and barks of whines at you.
Score 2. He knows you have the snack and tells you he wants it, but won't go looking for it.

If he stays in front of you, waiting patiently.
Score 1. He knows you have the treat, but doesn't show enough initiative to ask or get it himself.

If your dog comes to you and just shows he wants to cuddle or play, or looks around for something else he can do.
Score 0. It's not there anymore, why care? Out of sight out of mind.

TEST 6

Goal of the test:

Let's see how observant your dog is. Will they notice a beam of light moving around on the floor and will he respond to it?

Things you need:

- A darkened room
- A flashlight

Do the test:

1. Play a flashlight beam around on the floor in a darkened room. Mimic the beam as if it were a prey by moving it slowly on the floor, freezing it, then suddenly move it an inch or two, freezing it again, a sudden jerk to the right or left, freeze, a zigzag, left or right again, etc. etc.

Scoring:

If your dog comes to check out the flashlight itself.
Score 4. He knows it's the source of the beam of light on the floor. Very advanced thinking on his behalf!

If he chases the beam on the floor.
Score 2

If he sees the beam of light on the floor and watches it move around, but not chasing it.
Score 1

If he has absolutely no interest and pays it little to no attention.
Score 0

TEST 7

Goal of the test:

To measure your dog's observation skills. Will he notice other dogs on your computer or TV? Does he think they're real?

Things you need:

- A Television, Computer, Laptop or Tablet.

Do the test:

1. If you can find a "Lassie" episode you're set. But in case you can't, a video that includes a lot of scenes with other dogs is fine. You'll be able to find plenty online. Try and pick one with multiple dogs in various sizes. A single smaller dog is harder to see on screen for your dog.
2. Your dog should be either lying down or sitting beside you when you watch the video. Wait to see if he notices the other dog on the screen without you needing to point it out to him. Your dog might become aware once the dog on screen makes a sound.
3. If your dog seems totally oblivious to the dogs on screen after a couple of minutes, you may direct your dog's attention to it. If needed, rewind to a key scene where the dog on screen is barking. Point to the scene of turn your dog's head toward it but don't say anything like "See the doggie?" or "Where's the doggie?" or he might jump up, run to the door while barking and the test will be spoiled.

Scoring:

If your dog notices the dog on screen and is nosing or nuzzling it or peeking behind the screen to see if they are hiding behind it.
Score 3

If your dog sees the dog's on screen and either stares at them or even barks at the screen.
Score 2

If your dog becomes alert when the dog on screen makes a sound but doesn't seem to tie it in with the images on screen and ends up barking pretty randomly, runs or looks to the door.
Score 1

If your dog couldn't be any less interested and doesn't notice or respond to the images on screen, even when the dogs on screen bark.
Score 0

TEST 8

Goal of the test:

Testing your dog's problem-solving skills. Can your dog get over an obstacle and maneuver his way to get something he wants on the other side?

Things you need:

- A narrow hallway or narrow space
- A huge pile of pillows or blankets or both
- A helper
- A treat

Do the test:

1. Choose a narrow space in your house, preferably a hallway. In the center of this narrow space, pile a lot of pillows or blankets across it, blocking it. Make the pile deep and more importantly, high enough so that your dog can't simply hop over it but has to climb and clamber across it. It should be a real challenge for your dog. However, it should be stable enough so that he doesn't tumble too much when he's trying to climb it.
2. To start, pick the side which feels more "trapped" for your dog. For example: If there are nothing but bedrooms on one side of the hallway while on the other end it leads to a major open part of the house, start him on the side of the "bedrooms" of the pillows and blankets. This will provide much more incentive to leave the boring space into the more open one.
3. Have your helper hold your dog on the side you have chosen for him. You, naturally, are on the other side, calling your dog over and waving the treat.

Scoring:

If he immediately climbs over the blankets and pillows.
Score 5

If it takes him 10-30 seconds
Score 4

If it takes him 30-60 seconds
Score 3

If he makes a few attempts to clamber it, but keeps turning back and stopping and doesn't make it across within 60 seconds.
Score 2

If he starts whining or barking, but doesn't make much of an effort to climb and clamber across.
Score 1

If he just stays on his side and doesn't make an effort.
Score 0

TEST 9

Goal of the test:

Testing your dog's problem-solving skills by seeing if he can push open a door to get something he wants on the other side.

Things you need:

- A dog crate or room
- A treat

Do the test:

1. Put you dog in a crate or room and close the door, but do not latch it. Show your dog the treat and call him over.
2. If you don't have a crate and put your dog in a room, make sure it's a room with a door that opens **away** from him. After all, the objective of this test is to see if he will push a door **outward.** Since most room doors are solid and not see through, you cannot show your dog a treat, so you will have to call him and hope that he wants to come to you bad enough to push open the door.

Scoring:

If he pushes the door open and comes to you in 10 seconds or less.
Score 5

If he pushes the door and comes out in 10-30 seconds.
Score 4

If he pushes the door and comes out in 30-60 seconds.

Score 3

If he tries to push or paw the door, but doesn't come out in 60 seconds.
Score 2

If he starts barking or whining but makes no effort to push the door and get out.
Score 1

If he's content staying in the crate or room and makes no effort at all to come out.
Score 0

TEST 10

Goal of the test:

Same as test 9 but reverse! To see your dog's problem-solving skills, we will see if this time he can **pull** open a door to get what he wants on the other side. Pulling will be a lot more challenging.

Things you need:

- A dog crate or a room
- A treat

Do the test:

1. Make sure your dog watches as you place a treat **inside** his crate or a room. To make sure he can see it, make sure the treat is a bit larger this time. It can also be a favorite toy or even a bone.
2. Push the door close but just like before, do not latch it. Feel free to point out the treat or toy in order to encourage your dog to get it.
3. If you don't have a crate, like before, you can use a room. Place yourself inside of it and call him over. This time your dog will need to **pull** the door **toward** himself.

Scoring:

If he paws, pulls or noses the door open in 10 seconds or less.
Score 5

If he does it between 10-30 seconds.
Score 4

If he does it between 30-60 seconds.
Score 3

If your dog tries to get in by pawing, pulling or nosing the door, but doesn't do so within 60 seconds.
Score 2

If he starts barking or whining but makes no effort to pull the door and get in.
Score 1

If he's content staying outside the crate or room and makes no effort at all to open it.
Score 0

TEST 11

Goal of the test:

To see if your dog pays attention to human words and tone of voice. Will he pick out familiar words, even if they are spoken in an unfamiliar tone when you're not looking at him directly?

Things you need:

- A relaxed dog who is lying down.

Do the test:

1. Make sure your dog is lying down or sitting comfortably and relaxed.
2. Watch your dog from the corner of your eye without looking directly to your dog, say his name and ask if he wants to go for a walk or do another favorite activity he likes best for example :Go for a car ride, outside to the yard etc. etc. Use the words you usually use to entice your dog, but **NOT** the usual tone of voice you usually use. Try a monotone flat voice like a robot for example. And try to make it a sentence, not a question at the end of it. You may have to practice this a few times when your dog isn't present.

Scoring:

If your dig gets excited right away.
Score 3

If he gets a little bit excited, but noticeably less than usual because he's unsure and uncertain of the tone of voice you use.

Score 2

If he looks at you in an alert manner because he heard something familiar but isn't quite sure.
Score 1

If he doesn't seem to have heard anything he recognizes.
Score 0

TEST 12

Goal of the test:

We will measure your dog's observation skills and to test his problem-solving skills. Once given a choice of cans (soup can), does he remember under which soup can you placed the treat? Can he even tip the can over to get to the treat?

Things you need:

- One treat
- Two clean and empty cans (a soup can)
- A watch with a second hand or stop watch
- A helper

Do the test:

1. Have your helper stand five feet away from you while your helper holds your dog.
2. Hold up the two cans so your dog can see them then place them down on the floor in front of you, between you and your dog, with the cans about three feet apart from each other.
3. Hold up the treat so your dog can see it. Making sure your dog has his eyes on the treat, place under one of the cans.
4. Wait about 15 seconds before your helper releases your dog.

Scoring:

If your dog goes directly to the can under which you placed the treat, tips the can over and gets the treat within 30 seconds of time.
Score 4

If he goes directly to the can under which you placed the treat and starts nosing or pawing at it but doesn't succeed within 30 seconds.
Score 3

If he goes the wrong can, discovers the treat isn't there (By either sniffing or tipping the can over), then goes to the right can and gets the treat all within 30 seconds.
Score 2

If he goes back and forth between the two cans, pawing or nosing at both of them, but unable to get the treat within 30 seconds.
Score 1

If he makes absolutely no effort at all to get either the treat or completely ignores both cans.
Score 0

TEST 13

Goal of the test:

We will test your dog's problem solving skills. Can he figure out that the only way to reach you when you're on the opposite side of a fence is to find an opening and go through it to the other side? Even if finding that opening means running away from you for a distance?

Things you need:

- A see through chain link, wire or wood slated fence.
- A helper

Do the test:

1. Find a spot in a fence that your dog can see through. It will have to be high enough so that your dog can't jump over it. There also has to be a gate or opening in it and at least 30 feet of unbroken fence on one side of the gate. Preferably it should be a fence that your dog has not seen before so that your dog doesn't know where exactly the opening is.
2. Your helper has to hold your dog on one side of the fence, about 30 feet from the opening. If it is a gate, make sure the gate is open.
3. Climb over the fence to the other side of the dog. **You cannot use the opening or fence yourself otherwise your dog will learn where it is.** This would spoil the nature of this test. If you cannot climb the fence yourself, you can use the opening or gate, but you have to inform your helper to temporarily avert your dog's eyes so your dog won't see the opening.
4. Once on the other side, get about 50 feet away from the fence

and turn to your dog. Encourage your dog to come over to you by calling his name and clapping and whatever it is you usually do to call him over. **But, do not point at the opening.**

Scoring:

If your dog finds the opening within 1 minute.
Score 5

If your dog finds the opening within 2 minutes.
Score 4

If your dog runs back and forth along the closed section of the fence for 2 minutes, but never seems to find the opening.
Score 3

If your dog spends a lot of time just jumping at the fence.
Score 2

If your dog spends a few times jumping at the fence or running along the closed section back and forth, but gives up before 2 minutes and just stands there silently or while barking at you.
Score 1

If your dog makes no attempt to go over or around the fence at all.
Score 0

TEST 14

Goal of the test:

We will test your dog's response to changes in his environment, his problem-solving skills and his memory. If you move your dog's food bowl to another room, will he remember after 5 minutes have passed? And if you cover your dog's food bowl with a newspaper or magazine, will he figure out how to get to his food?

Things you need:

- A newspaper or magazine
- Your dog's food bowl, filled with food
- A helper

Do the test:

1. When your dog's normal feeding time occurs, place your dog's bowl, filled with his usual dog food, in a room in which you've never put it before. Preferably in the furthest corner of that room away from the door.
2. Take your dog to see his bowl and let him smell it. You can even let him have a bite or two. After that, take your dog outdoors and play with him for a couple of minutes. Meanwhile, have your helper place a magazine or newspaper on top of your dog's food bowl, completely covering it.
3. When you bring your dog back in from playing, take him to the room where he usually eats his food and release him. Start a timer. Give him 60 seconds to figure it out.

Scoring:

If your dog heads straight to the room where his bowl is and pushes off the newspaper or magazine so he can start eating right away.
Score 7

If your dog sniffs around his usual feeding room but eventually gets to the room the food bowl has been placed in and pushes off the newspaper or magazine within 60 seconds.
Score 6

If your dog heads straight to the room where his bowl is, and starts pawing or nosing the newspaper or magazine but isn't able to push it off within 60 seconds.
Score 5

If your dog starts sniffing around his usual feeding room and eventually gets to the correct room, and starts pawing or nosing the newspaper or magazine but isn't able to push it off within 60 seconds.
Score 4

If your dog goes straight to the room where the bowl is, but only makes little effort or no attempt at all to push off the magazine or newspaper within 60 seconds.
Score 3

If your dog starts sniffing around his usual feeding room and eventually gets to the correct room, but only makes little effort or no attempt at all to push off the magazine or newspaper within 60 seconds.
Score 2

If your dog stands around the usual feeding spot, looking at you wondering where the bowl is and never looks elsewhere within 60 seconds.
Score 1

If your dog seems to have forgotten that there ever was food or a food bowl and simply wanders off or lies down or starts to play with something and 60 seconds have gone by.
Score 0

TEST 15

Goal of the test:

We will test your dog's response to human social signals. Will your dog recognize and interpret human moods and emotions correctly?

Things you need:

- You most amazing acting skills

Do the test:

1. With your dog closely by your side, sit on your couch and pretend to be very sad. Put the saddest expression you can muster on your face, sob into your hands, wipe your eyes and blow your nose. Notice your dog's reaction to it (See scoring charts below). Then reassure your dog and play with him for a little while.
2. An hour later, while your dog is closely by your side again, settle down on the couch or chair with a book. After a few minutes, pretend your book is the most hilarious thing you've ever read. Smile broadly, giggle, chuckle and laugh out loud. Note your dog's reaction again.
3. After another hour, while your dog is closely by your side again, pretend to be irritated. Your face should look annoyed. Put your hands on your hips and stump around the house, scolding and muttering under your breath. Note your dog's reaction again and then reassure him. Perhaps a tasty little treat may help and play with him for a while.

Scoring:

If you dog responded to all three of you moods, for example, consoling and concerned when you were sad, playful or happy when you were laughing and watchful or nervous when you were angry.
Score 3

If your dog responded to two of your moods.
Score 2

If your dog responded to one of your mood.
Score 1

If he couldn't care any less about any of your moods.
Score 0

TEST 16

Goal of the test:

We will test how observant your dog is. Will he recognize a common household items and associate it with a routine, like going for a walk?

Things you need:

- Your keys
- Your jacket
- Your leash
- A relaxed, sitting or lying down dog

Do the test:

1. You choose a room where your dog likes to lie down, but where he can clearly see the door you usually use when you take him out for a walk
2. Now, put your dog in another room or outside so he cannot see what you might be doing. Take you're three items (Keys, leash and jacket) and group them together somewhere in the room a good distance from where you dog likes to lie down and a good distance from the door.
   For example: Form a triangle with three points about the same distance apart. The door, the place where you placed the three items and your dog's usual resting place.
3. Now you let your dog back into the room. Simply sit and find something casual to do, like reading a book. You want to use this time to give your dog time to settle down, relax and perhaps lie down. Ideally he will sit or lie down across the room from the door and also across the room from the items.

4. Now that your dog is hopefully settled and relaxed, watch him from the corner of your eye. When he happens to glance in your direction, stand up. Without looking at your dog walk to your three items (Jacket, keys, leash). Pick up your jacket and put it on. Then pick up the keys and after that, the leash. **Do not look at your dog.** Eye contact might encourage him to come over and it might spoil the test.

5. Now **stop** where you are and everything you're doing. Stand perfectly still, and don't move toward the door.

Scoring:

If your dog comes to you instantly, flies of the sofa as soon as you reached for your jacket or if he goes to the door or everything all at once.
Score 4

Otherwise, walk to the door while still not looking at your dog and stop in front of the door. If your dog comes now.
Score 3

If your dog still hasn't come to you, place your hand on the doorknob and wiggle or rattle it. If your dog comes to you now.
Score 2

If your dog still hasn't come to you but is looking interested and alert to you.
Score 1

If your dog is paying you no attention at all.
Score 0

TEST 17

Goal of the test:

We will do the (Soup) can test again like we did in <u>test 12</u> but this time with only one can. We will test your dog's problem-solving skills. Will he notice you placing a treat under the can and will he remember the treat is there even when he can no longer see it? Can he figure out how to tip the can over to get to it?

Things you need:

- One treat
- A clean, empty soup can
- A watch with a second hand or a stopwatch
- A helper

Do the test:

1. Make sure you show your dog the treat to make him excited. Then tuck it in your fist and let him sniff it for a good few seconds.
2. Now place the treat on the floor, making sure your dog sees your actions. A helper might want to hold your dog back when you do this. Now place the empty soup can over it and step back a few steps.
3. Let your helper release your dog at the same time you start the timer. Encourage your dog to get the treat with words for example "Where is it?" or "Find it, get it!" but do not point him in the right direction by tapping the floor or pointing at the can. He is supposed to notice where you put the treat on his own.

Scoring:

If your dog tips the can and is able to get the treat within 5 seconds.
Score 5

If your dog tips the can and gets the treat in 5-15 seconds.
Score 4

If your dog tips the can and gets the treat in 15-30 seconds.
Score 3

If your dog tips the can and gets the treat in 30-60 seconds.
Score 2

If your dog tries at least a couple of time to pawing or nosing at the can but doesn't succeed within 60 seconds.
Score 1

If your dog makes absolutely no effort to get the treat within 60 seconds.
Score 0

TEST 18

Goal of the test:

We will test how curious and observant your dog is. We will see if he will notice when you drastically rearrange the furniture in a familiar room and see if he explores all the changes.

Things you need:

- A stopwatch or watch with a second hand
- A rearranged room

Do the test:

1. Bring your dog outside so he will not notice the changes to the room that you are about to make.
2. Pick a room your dog is very familiar with. It's time to rearrange the furniture in that room. This might take some effort, but make sure you rearrange at least five furniture pieces. Not simple picture frames or adding a plant, but make the change dramatic. Move a sofa to another wall, turn the TV in another direction, put a chair or table upside down. Make it look completely different.
3. Bring your dog inside and into the rearranged room and start your timer. Stand there quietly and do not say a word to your dog. Do not reassure him in any way and do not touch your dog. Nor should you look directly at your dog to observe him. Just watch him in silence form the corner of your eye.

Scoring:

If your dog notices that something is different within 5 seconds and starts to check out one of the changes by sniffing curiously or cautiously at it and extending his neck while doing so.
Score 5

If your dog notices and checks out at least one of the changes within 5-15 seconds.
Score 4

If your dog notices and checks out at least one of the changes within 15-30 seconds.
Score 3

If your dog appears cautious as if he noticed the changes but not willing to approach them or sniffing them within 30 seconds of time.
Score 2

If your dog is so suspicious of the changes in the room that he backs away or runs away and won't come back in the room on his own (do not pressure or coax him) within 30 seconds.
Score 1

If your dog doesn't notice any changes and everything appears to be normal to him within 30 seconds of time.
Score 0

TEST 19

Goal of the test:

We will measure how observant your dog is and how correctly he will respond to human social signals. Will he notice when you smile and will he interpret it as meaning that you're happy?

Things you need:

- A relaxed sitting or lying down dog.

Do the test:

1. Wait for a time when your dog is relaxed, comfortable and either lying down or sitting. He is preferably 8 feet away from you. You might be doing something like reading, working on your computer or laptop or doing dishes.
2. Not saying anything to attract your dog's attention but watching your dog from the corner of your eye, wait for him to look directly at you. Once he looks at you, look back at him and smile a huge broad exaggerated smile.

Scoring:

If your dog comes to you happily.
Score 4

If your dog stays where he is but barks at you or wags his tail.
Score 4

If your dog comes half way to you but stops somewhere in the middle, as though he's uncertain.

Score 3

If your dog stays where he is and looks alert at you, clearly focused on your face but not making a sound or wagging his tail.
Score 2

If your dog gets up and moves away from you or walks into another room because although he saw your facial expression, he didn't interpret it correctly.
Score 1. At least he noticed it.

If your dog pays your smile no attention at all and keeps being in the same spot.
Score 0

TEST 20

Goal of the test:

We will measure your dog's problem-solving skills by placing a treat underneath a towel and see if he will notice. Will he remember that the treat is there even if he can no longer see it? Is he able to manipulate the towel in such a way that he can get to the treat?

Things you need:

- One treat
- A hand or dish towel (but not a big bath towel)
- A stopwatch or watch with a second hand
- Perhaps a helper

Do the test:

1. Make sure you show your dog the treat. Tuck it into your fist and let him sniff it for a good few seconds so your dog gets excited about the treat.
2. Now place the treat on the floor, making sure your dog sees this action. Your helper might want to hold your dog for this. Now, lay the hand or dish towel over it and step back a few steps from the towel.
3. Have your helper let go of your dog and start the timer at the same time. Feel free to encourage your dog to get the treat by saying "Where is the treat?" or "Find it! Get it!" But do not touch or point your dog in the right direction nor should you tap or touch the towel to make your dog aware of where the treat is. He is supposed to find and notice it on his own.

Scoring:

If your dog manages to get under the towel and get the treat within 15 seconds.
Score 5

If your dog does it in 15-30 seconds.
Score 4

If your dog does it in 30-60 seconds.
Score 3

If your dog does it in 1-2 minutes.
Score 2

If your dog tries at least a couple of times to get his treat by nosing or pawing at the towel but does not succeed within 2 minutes.
Score 1

If your dog makes no effort at all to get the treat within 2 minutes.
Score 0

TEST 21

Goal of the test:

This test comes in two parts. Do this test, test 21 and test 22 one after another. First this test 21 and then immediately after, test 22.

We will test and measure your dog's memory. Will he remember where you have placed a treat even if he is removed from the room for 10 seconds?

Things you need:

- **Two** treats
- The Dog's leash
- A stopwatch or a watch with a second hand
- A helper

Do the test:

1. Choose a room that doesn't have much furniture in it. The room itself needs to be average sized.
2. Have your helper hold your dog in the center of this room. You then show your dog the treat. Now close your hand with the snack in it into a fist and let your dog sniff it for a good 5 seconds so he gets excited about it.
3. Walk to a corner of the room but make sure it's the furthest from the door. Now call your dog's attention to the treat and place the treat on the floor, making sure your dog sees this action. And say something like "Look, a treat! Here it is!"
4. Now take your dog from your helper and leave the room, leading it into another room. Walk with your dog for about 10 seconds around in this new room. Then bring him back to the

door.

5.   Start your timer, let go of your dog and encourage him to get the treat, but **do not** point at the treat.

Scoring:

If your dog goes straight toward the treat.
Score 4

If your dog sniffs determinedly around the room, clearly trying to sniff out the treat and finds it within 30 seconds.
Score 3

If your dog is clearly looking for it, but it wasn't found within 30 seconds.
Score 2

If your dog wanders vaguely around and accidentally stumbles upon the treat.
Score 1

If your dog makes no effort to get the treat within 30 seconds.
Score 0

Now, immediately do the next test, using the other treat.

TEST 22

Goal of the test:

We will now start the second part of the test in which we will test your dog's long-term memory. Will your dog remember where you placed the treat, even after 5 minutes have passed?

Things you need:

- The other treat
- Your dog's leash
- A stopwatch or watch with a second hand
- A helper

Do the test:

1. Same as before, have your helper hold your dog in the center of the room and show your dog the second treat and let him smell it when you have your fist closed.
2. Now, walk into a different corner of the room that you used in the previous test. Call attention to your dog making absolutely sure that he sees you place it on the floor.
3. Again, it's time to lead your dog out of the room into a different room or outside. This time play with him or walk him around for a good 5 minutes. After 5 minutes have passed, lead him back in and back to the door of the room.
4. Start your time and release your dog and once again, encourage him to find the treat.

Scoring:

If your dog goes straight toward the treat.
Score 4

If your dog goes to the corner where the first treat was in test 21, then quickly and directly goes to the correct corner.
Score 3

If your dog sniffs all around the room, clearly looking for the treat and finding it within 45 seconds.
Score 2

If your dog wanders vaguely around and accidentally stumbles upon the treat.
Score 1

If your dog makes no effort to get the treat within 45 seconds.
Score 0

TEST 23

Goal of the test:

We will measure your dog's problem-solving skills by seeing if he can figure out that he can't reach a treat under a low table unless he uses his paw to pull it out from underneath it.

Things you need:

- A very low standing table or a table-like structure under which you can tuck a treat that the dog must pull out with his paw
- A hard treat that your dog can easily pull out with his paw
- A stopwatch or watch with a second hand

Do the test:

1. If you have a table, chair or sofa that is close enough to the ground so your dog's head can't fit under it, but his paw can fit under it (two or three inches clearance works for most small to medium-sized dogs), this will work just fine.

   Otherwise, we will have to build such a structure, which is not difficult.

   Have two stacks of large heavy books or "legs" and place a heavy board on top of them. Weight the board down with an extra few books or heavy objects so your dog won't be able to push or nuzzle the board off.

   Please make sure your dog can't get his head underneath the structure otherwise he'll simply grab the tasty treat with his mouth.

2. Now, Make sure you show your dog the treat, tuck it into a closed fist and let him sniff it for a good 5 seconds so your dog will start getting excited about it.
3. Now, tuck the tasty treat under your low structure. Push it far enough underneath it so he can't reach it with his mouth but close enough for him to reach it with his paw. It may take a few attempts and trial and error to get the distance just right. If you need to do this one over again because the distance wasn't right because the treat was to close and your dog managed to snag it with his teeth, or if it was too far away for your dog to reach with his paw, it's alright.

   If at certain times your dog hits the treat with his paw, pushing it out of his reach, use your hand to pull it within his reach again. You will want to give him a fair chance of pulling it out from underneath the table, couch or structure.
4. Start the timer and feel free to encourage your dog to get the treat.

Scoring:

If your dog uses his paw to retrieve the treat within 60 seconds.
Score 5

If your dog uses his paw to retrieve the treat in 1-3 minutes.
Score 4

If your dog is persistent in trying to use his paw in order to retrieve the treat, but hasn't succeeded in doing so within 3 minutes.
Score 3

If your dog is persistent in trying to get the treat, but instead of his paw he only uses his nose and muzzle.
Score 2

If your dog only makes a few token attempts to get the treat with his nose, muzzle or paw, but gives up within a minute.
Score 1

If your dog makes no effort to get the treat within 3 minutes.

Score 0

TEST 24

Goal of the test:

We will measure how quickly your dog learns a new word and how many repetitions it takes before he can actually do it.

Things you need:

- Many treats. At least 20 pieces should do
- Your dog's leash

Do the test:

1. We will teach your dog the phrase "Come Front" and hopefully he hasn't learned it yet. "Come Front" means your dog should get up from a heel position (sitting on your left side), take a couple of steps forward and turn to face you and sit in front of you, facing you.
2. On to teaching him! With your dog on a leash and sitting at your left side and with a pocket full of treat, give the command "Come Front!"
   With both hands, pat your legs just above your knees as a hand signal.
3. Now it's time to show your dog what the new command means. Step forward with your right foot and use the leash to encourage you dog to step forward with you.
4. Once your dog is up and moving, step backward with your right foot so you end up back where you started. At the same time while you do so, use the leash to turn your dog clockwise toward you, so he is in front of you while facing you. If you have a larger dog, you may have to take an additional step back

to give him a little more room to turn and face you.

5. Now, use your hands to sit your dog down in front of your knees, facing you. Do not say the words "sit", just place him in a sitting position with your hands.
   You want this to become a smooth routine of motion of rise, step forward, turn, face you, and sit. All done in one single phrase: "Come Front." There is no need to complicate it further by adding other words like "sit."

6. Once your dog sits in front of you, praise him and reward him with a treat. Once he has eaten his treat, place him back in the heel position, sitting on the left side of your leg and repeat the whole teaching process **four** more times.

7. Now it is time to test your dog. After five complete routines of this, put him back in the heel position on the left side of your leg. Say, "Come Front." But this time **don't** step forward and **don't** move the leash.

Scoring:

If your dog rises, turns toward you and sits (even if he does it in a sloppy or crooked manner), he might be, at least on this specific test, a genius.
Score 6

If your dog doesn't do anything or stands up but doesn't turn to face you or if he comes around to face you but doesn't sit, don't worry. This is normal behavior. Guide your dog through the correct motions again so that he does end up in the correct front position. Praise and give him another treat. Then repeat the original training process again where you step forward and backward with your leg, guide him with the leash and sit your dog down in front of you with your hands for more times like before. And try it again this time. If on his second time of this test he assumes the correct front position. **Score 5.** This is still very, very good.

If after two tries, your dog still won't assume the correct position, help him to achieve it again. And then repeat the training process again 4 times and try the test again. If on his third time doing the test he assumes the correct position.
Score 4

If your dog, after training three times still won't assume the correct position, help him to achieve it again. Then repeat the training another four more times and try the test again. If on his fourth time he assumes the correct position.
Score 3

If your dog, after training four times and learning the new word 20 times, still hasn't assumed the correct position, give him credit for whatever part of the routine he did do right. If he's coming around or to the front and facing you, but not sitting.
Score 2

If your dog simply stands up when you say "Come Front." But not actually coming to the front to face you.
Score 1. You dog is at least aware that the word means he is supposed to do something.

If your dog continues to sit and does absolutely nothing or just stares at you.
Score 0

TEST 25

Goal of the test:

We will measure your dog's problem-solving skills. We will see if your dog can figure out that the only way to get a treat on the other side of a high enough barrier is to go around the barrier.

Things you need:

- A treat
- A barrier
- A helper
- A stopwatch or watch with second hand

Do the test:

1. In this test for your dog we will be required to do some minor construction. In order to create the barrier we will need a large piece of cardboard, three or four feet wide and high enough so your dog cannot jump over it. You can tape pieces of cardboard together if you need to.
2. At the center of this cardboard barrier, cut out a vertical opening. Start cutting this opening a couple of inches from the bottom of the cardboard and ending a couple of inches from the top. This opening should be about three inches wide.
3. Prop up this cardboard barrier by taping it to two additional pieced of cardboard or you could attach the cardboard to two boxes, or chairs laid on their sides.
4. Now, have your always helpful helper hold your dog in front of the cardboard barrier. You will then go behind the barrier, crouching down, and attract your dog's attention so he looks at

you through the three inch wide vertical slit you've made.

5. Draw your dog's attention through this 'window' by holding a treat for him. But hold it just out of reach of his paw.

6. Now, have your helper release your dog and start your timer at the same time. Don't say a word to encourage your dog. Your dog will have to figure out what he will have to do himself if he wants the treat.

Scoring:

If your dog goes around the barrier and gets the treat within 10 seconds.
Score 5

If your dog goes around the barrier and gets the treat within 10-20 seconds.
Score 4

If your dog goes around the barrier and gets the treat within 20-30 seconds.
Score 3

If your dog goes around the barrier and gets the treat within 30-60 seconds.
Score 2

If your dog tries to reach through the little vertical 'window' with his nose or paw but doesn't attempt to go around the barrier.
Score 1

If your dog makes no effort to get the treat within 60 seconds.
Score 0

THE SCORE RESULTS!

Now it is time to add up all the points your dog may have scored. The highest possible score for your dog is 111 points.

In the graph below you can see the results of your dog once you have added up all the points your dog has scored.

Total Points	Percentage	Rating	IQ
106-111	96-100%	Genius	140+
95-105	86-95%	Superior	125-140
84-94	76-85%	Above Average	105-125
73-83	66-75%	Average	95-105
51-72	46-65%	Below Average	70-95
33-50	30-45%	Deficient	60-70
Less than 33	Less than 30%	Brain Dead?	Less than 60

IF YOUR DOG SCORED HIGH.

If your dog scored high on the test, you may be wondering why or perhaps you already know why your dog scored high.

You may be surprised by this but "high scoring" and "smart" do not automatically mean the same thing. There may be other reasons why your dog scored so high.

He may have had previous training.

He may have done well because he might have had some previous training. In other words, he may have done well because of you. Like many people, if you taught your dog his name, you taught your dog to listen to you and I can only congratulate you on that. Training takes effort and since you taught your dog his name, he is accustomed to paying attention and working with you. All these experiences took time and helped him get a higher score than normal.

His higher score may reflect your skill and persistence rather than his innate intelligence, but rest assured, your teaching methods and efforts have made him smarter! The simple acts of teaching and training your dog develops his brain and makes him much more successful at doing new things and learning new commands.

You should make an effort to teach him more new things. Now that you have seen the results of a little training, you can do a whole lot more with your dog to boost his intelligence, attentiveness, and responsiveness by teaching him more commands.

He is eager to please.

He may have also done very well because your dog is eager to please. A dog who is eager to please his owner will double his efforts on each test. Because of that, your dog will score higher than a dog with greater raw intelligence but no desire to please.

This kind of personality is far more important than intelligence, especially when it comes to training. It will ease the process of learning new commands and routines.

Continue to train your dog, it will satisfy your dog's eagerness to please. By teaching him new words and commands it will satisfy him by getting the praise and rewards he craves from you.

He is indeed very smart.

If your dog is indeed very smart, it may or may not be a good thing. As I've said before, personality is more important than intelligence when it comes to the ease of training. If however, your dog is not only smart, but also very eager to please, it's a wonderful and terrific thing! He is both willing and able to learn new things.

However, if your dog is smart and also stubborn, independent, strong-willed or dominant, this is far from good and his high intelligence may make it even worse. He may be using his clever reasoning skills to do things you don't want him to do, for example, figuring out how to open a gate or door or the cookie cabinet.

But because he's so smart and clever, it can be beneficial to get him through an excellent and good manners training program. This way your dog will learn that even though he would like to go his own way and do his own things, there are certain things he must adhere to and be well-behaved.

Whatever your dog's personality may be, if you don't keep your smart dog busy and don't teach him new words, commands and behaviors to keep his mind stimulated, he might be getting into trouble.

- Smart dogs get bored very easily.
- Smart dogs are always looking for challenges, interesting things to do and stimulation.
- Smart dogs like to go for walks in new unexplored places, meet

new people, play with new toys, learn new words and solve new puzzles.

- Smart dogs must be kept entertained and interested. If you do too much of the same things with your dog, they will look for other ways to amuse and entertain themselves like destroying furniture, digging holes in your yard for example.
  Smart dogs will learn very quickly which behaviors bring them the most attention which unfortunately means that doing something "bad" will get them a lot of attention.

Thus, keep your smart dog busy and entertained. Train with them, teach them new words and behaviors. This way you will be keeping your dog busy and mentally sharp!

IF YOUR DOG SCORED LOW.

If your dog scored low and seems to be a not-so-smart one. Don't worry, low-scoring and not-so-smart don't automatically mean the same thing. There may be other reasons your dog scored low on the tests.

You don't have the right relationship with your dog.

One of the reasons may be because you don't have the right relationship with your dog. At least, not yet. If your dog doesn't seem to listen to you, doesn't pay attention to you, doesn't respond to his name when you call him or pays you no attention. Then in that case it is hard to determine whether it's his failure to do the test is because he simply can't or because you haven't developed the proper "Leader-Follower" relationship so that he works with you.

You will have to have the proper "leader-Follower" relationship with your dog if you hope to train your dog. You need to change your relationship with your dog so he does listen to you, does pay attention to you and does respond to you when you tell him to do things. Learn how to assume the leading role in your relationship with your dog. You will love the change and your dog will love and respect you for it.

He doesn't care about treats or toys.

Your dog may have not done well because your dog isn't food or toy oriented at all. It is hard to motivate your dog and test or train him if he has absolutely no interest in either toys or treats. This throws a wrench into things since toys or treats are offered as reward in most types of training. However, your dog might be more responsive to your voice or petting as rewards.

He is timid of trying new things.

Your dog might be timid, suspicious of new changes or reluctant to do anything out of the ordinary. Your dog might be afraid to even try a test. Timid and rigid dogs don't usually adjust well to normal things that life throws at them, especially not when it comes to training new behaviors and testing them. However, self-confidence and mental flexibility can be, like most things, taught. Once trained properly, your dog will learn so many new things that his self-esteem will be greatly boosted and he will be more willing to accept new things and behaviors more easily.

He has a specific type of intelligence.

Most dogs are generally bright and capable of learning virtually anything. It may be that your dog has very strong abilities in one limited and specific area. He may be good at herding livestock, guarding, hunting bird or game animals or pulling sleds. But won't learn very well or solve problems outside of that specific field.

If your dog is one of those dogs that are good at herding, hunting, guarding etc. Which means his strong instincts are hardwired into his genes which may not adopt well in a home environment where his working behaviors are not at all possible or valued and may even be considered a nuisance by you or your family.

However, just because he has these very specific working instincts embedded into him, it does not mean you cannot train him. You will just have to use his instinctual skills for teaching. You can still train him in canine activities such as field work, herding, sledding, carting, coursing, luring, guarding and much, much more and keep him active with these training methods so he won't become a nuisance at home.

He is indeed not very smart it seems.

If your dog is indeed not very smart, this may be good or simply just fine. Remember, personality is far more important than intelligence when it comes to the ease of training your dog.

He may be eager to please which is always good. The training might go slower than usual, but your dog is very willing to learn. The not so smart dog, paired with the right personality, can make a very fine companion. Your dog will often thrive in a normal household where much of his life is repetitive and predicable where very smart dogs would probably go crazy with such 'boring' routines.

Training your not so smart dog may take a lot of time but it's absolutely not impossible. The goal is to teach him that those funny sounds you make with your mouth (commands) have meaning. And that responding appropriately to them will lead to a reward. You will, in essence, teach your dog how to learn. Once you've taught him that, it will almost always lead automatically lead to a smarter dog who is able to learn other things. It is a snowball effect. Once he's learned that commands and listening to them will get him a reward, his skill and intelligent will start to snowball with this very first thing you just taught him.

If, however, your not so smart dog is also independent, dominant **AND** stubborn, it might be really bad. He not only learns very slowly, but also has no willingness to learn. In order to bring this difficult personality under control, it is imperative that you get him through an excellent good manners program so he can learn that even though he would prefer to do his own thing, there are certain things he must do to be well-behaved and thus rewarded.

IF YOUR DOG SCORED AVERAGE.

Your dog seems to have joined the club where most dogs reside. Completely average is not a bad score at all. The more important question is what his personality is like. Personality is the real key to success when it comes to training and learning new behaviors. Personality determines how easy or how hard it will be when you start to train him.

If your average intelligent dog is eager to please, then he will make a very fine companion. To satisfy your dog's eagerness to please, you can teach him lots of new words and behaviors. Especially because eager to please dogs crave praise and rewards. And you will also be pleased to discover that the very act of training him and teaching new things will develop his brain even further and boost his intelligence higher.

If your average intelligent dog is stubborn, independent or strong willed, you may have some work to do. Don't worry though. As always, not only will you be rewarded, but your dog too. To bring his difficult personality under control you will have to go through an excellent good manner program. Your dog will learn that even though he would prefer to do his own things and go his own way, there are certain things he must do to be well behaved and thus rewarded.